BRIDGING THE ENERGY GAP

Andrew Langley

Chicago, Illinois

www.heinemannraintree.com

Visit our website to find out more information about Heinemann-Raintree books.

To order:

☎ Phone 888-454-2279

🖳 Visit www.heinemannraintree.com to browse our catalog and order online.

Edited by Andrew Farrow and Adam Miller
Designed by Victoria Allen
Original illustrations © Capstone Global Library Ltd.
Illustrated by Tower Designs UK Limited
Picture research by Mica Brancic
Production by Camilla Crask
Originated by Capstone Global Library
Printed and bound in China by South China Printing Company.

15 14 13 12 11
10 9 8 7 6 5 4 3 2 1

Library of Congress Cataloging-in-Publication Data
Langley, Andrew, 1949-
  Bridging the energy gap / Andrew Langley.
    p. cm.—(The environment challenge)
  Includes bibliographical references and index.
  ISBN 978-1-4109-4297-5 (hardback)—ISBN 978-1-4109-4304-0 (pbk.) 1. Renewable energy sources—Juvenile literature. I. Title.
  TJ808.2.L36 2012
  333.79—dc22   2010052705

ISBNs: 978-1-4109-4297-5 (HC); 978-1-4109-4304-0 (PB)

Acknowledgments

The author and publishers are grateful to the following for permission to reproduce copyright material: Corbis p. 4 © Rudy Sulgan. p.20 © Ed Kashi, p. 22 epa/Pool/© Sebastian Derungs, p. 23 © Karen Kasmauski, p. 25 © Francesco Acerbis, p. 26 © Cameron Davidson, p. 29 epa/© Song Jianchun, p.30 © Layne Kennedy, p.31 Robert Harding World Imagery/© David Lomax, p.32 Science Faction/© Peter Ginter, p. 35 epa/© Alex Hofford, p. 36 Reuters/© Brian Snyder, p. 41 Aurora Photos/© Peter Essick; Getty Images p. 5 U.S. Coast Guard, p. 7 Taxi/Allan Shoemake, p. 10 Photographer's Choice/Lester Lefkowitz, p. 11 Bloomberg/Norm Betts, p. 12 Hulton Archive/Fox Photos, p. 15 AFP Photo/Frederic J. Brown, p. 17 Spencer Platt, p. 33 David McNew, p. 34 AFP Photo/Frederick Florin, p. 37 Tim Graham, p. 38 Eco Images/Universal Images Group p. 39 Visuals Unlimited, Inc./Ashley Cooper, p. 40 AFP Photo DDP/Hero Lang; Reuters p. 8 © Krishnendu Halder; Science Photo Library p. 19 David Nunik; Shutterstock p. 24 © John Carnemolla, p. 18 © Philip Lange.

Cover photograph of a resident collecting pieces of wood washed ashore in front of wind turbines in the Philippines used with permission of Reuters/© Cheryl Ravelo.

We would like to thank Michael D. Mastrandrea, Ph.D. for his invaluable help in the preparation of this book.

Every effort has been made to contact copyright holders of any material reproduced in this book. Any omissions will be rectified in subsequent printings if notice is given to the publisher.

Contents

Words appearing in the text in bold, **like this**, are explained in the glossary.

Powering the World

Energy is all around us. It comes into our houses in the form of electricity, which makes light and powers all sorts of machines, from dishwashers and refrigerators to televisions and computers. Energy also enters our homes as the gas or oil that is used to heat our air and water and to cook our food. There are more kinds of energy outdoors, which you can feel from natural forces such as the wind, the movement of the sea, and the heat and light of the Sun.

Energy at work

So, what is energy? It is the ability to do work. When you run or jump or play soccer, you get hot. This is because your body is working hard and using up its energy supplies. You also get hot when you sit by a fire. In this example, it is the fire that is working and using up energy to create heat.

Energy is what keeps our world working. In power stations, the energy from fuel sources such as coal or oil is released to produce enormous supplies of electricity. This powers factory machines, radio transmitters, streetlights, and electric trains. Other kinds of fuel, like gasoline and diesel, drive aircraft, tractors, trucks, and cars.

Modern cities use a huge amount of energy. In the form of electricity, it lights thousands of buildings, street lamps, and signs.

The energy gap

But this way of living cannot go on forever. Why not? There are two big energy problems facing the world:

1. Many of these resources will run out one day. There is only a limited supply of important materials such as coal, oil, and **natural gas**, a fuel gas found naturally in the ground. When we have used them up, there will be no more.

2. When coal or oil burn, they release a substance called **carbon** into the air. The level of carbon is rising rapidly, and is the major cause of the dangerous rise in the world's temperatures that is known as **global warming**. We have to find safer ways to create power.

These problems are growing fast. Soon, they may create an "**energy gap**," meaning a situation in which we cannot produce enough power for our needs.

Solving the problem

We are already using other sources of energy that will never run out, such as flowing water, the wind, and the Sun. Scientists are developing more methods of unlocking the energy of the natural world. Will these be enough? This book will help you explore the options and make your own decisions about how to bridge the energy gap.

Smoke and flames above an oil leak from a drilling rig. Accidents like this can badly damage the environment.

The energy chain

Most sources of energy occur naturally. Coal, oil, and natural gas lie underground, while wind, water, and sunshine are above the surface. These are all called the **primary sources** of energy. But we cannot use them directly. For example, how could you heat yourself with wind, or power your computer with a lump of coal?

These primary sources have to be turned into the sort of energy we can use at home or at work. For example, coal is burned, and the heat is then used to create electricity. Wind and water turn machines called **turbines**, which also create electricity.

What does it cost?

It takes a lot of work to convert raw energy sources into **secondary sources**, meaning sources of power we can use. For example, coal, oil, and natural gas have to be carried long distances to places called plants, where they can be turned into usable forms of energy. And giant turbines have to be built to use wind power.

Coal, oil, and natural gas have to be carried long distances to plants, where they can be turned into usable fuels.

The energy then has to be distributed to customers. Look in the street. Can you see cables carrying electrical power? Or covers in the road where gas and water pipes run beneath your feet? Other underground cables bring television and cable connections. All this costs customers a lot of money.

Electricity is distributed to customers along huge networks, or grids, of cables.

Looking for evidence

How can you find out more about energy and its future? To make a balanced judgment, you need evidence—facts, figures, images, and expert opinions. Here are some places to look:

- Libraries have books of all kinds, as well as DVDs and databases of information, such as news articles.

- The Internet offers a huge choice of sites and opinions about energy, fuels, and the environment.

- Newspapers, radio, and television often feature stories about the future of energy.

WORD BANK

nuclear energy	energy made by splitting the nucleus (central part) of a uranium atom
primary source	first or original source of energy, such as the wind
secondary source	source of power that can be used, such as electricity
turbine	machine that is turned by flowing energy, such as water, and that converts this energy into electricity

A growing world

The world's **population** (number of people) is growing at an amazing speed. Back in 1950, there were about 2.5 billion people on Earth. By 2010 the total had reached 6.9 billion. Some people estimate it will reach 8.5 billion by 2025. On top of this, the **economies** (management of money and other resources) in countries such as China and India are expanding rapidly as new factories, towns, and transportation systems are built.

Rapid economic growth has meant an increase in the number of cars—and traffic jams—in many countries.

This explosion of growth means that more and more energy will be needed in years to come. Demand for primary and secondary sources throughout the world is likely to rise by more than 30 percent in the next 20 years.

How long will our resources last?

A look at the pie chart on the right shows just how much we depend on the **fossil fuels** oil, coal, and natural gas to **generate** (create) energy. These three energy sources account for more than three-quarters of the world's energy.

But where do fossil fuels come from? They began as the remains of ancient plants and animals. (The remains are called fossils.) Over millions of years, these fossils were crushed underground and changed into fossil fuels.

But when are these materials going to run out? Nobody knows the exact answer to this question. One expert, Hermann-Josef Wagner, has predicted that oil will last 40 to 50 more years, coal will last 180 to 240 more years, and natural gas will last 50 to 60 more years.

How accurate are these figures? See if you can find other experts' predictions that give a different picture. To start with, try www.scienceonline.co.uk/energy/nonrenewable.html.

"The Sun provides Earth with as much energy every hour as human civilization uses every year."

Nature magazine, 2006

A global energy pie chart

A pie chart is a simple way of showing how a total is divided up into parts. In a pie chart, a circle represents the total. From above, it looks like a pie, with each part becoming a slice of the whole. This pie chart shows approximately how much of each kind of energy source the world uses.

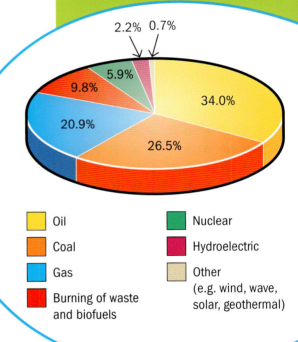

2.2% 0.7%
5.9%
9.8%
20.9%
34.0%
26.5%

Oil
Coal
Gas
Burning of waste and biofuels
Nuclear
Hydroelectric
Other (e.g. wind, wave, solar, geothermal)

You can get lots of energy statistics and information for yourself by looking on the website of the International Energy Authority at www.iea.org and clicking on "Statistics," then "Key statistics."

Where Does Energy Come From?

We cannot create **energy** out of nothing. All the energy in the world has to be released from a source, such as coal or oil. These resources are already here on Earth. But where did the energy come from to make them in the first place? The answer is simple: the Sun.

Linked to the Sun

Almost all our energy comes from the Sun. You can show this by drawing a chart like the one here. On one side of the chart is the Sun itself. On the other side are the many things that need **solar energy**, meaning energy from the Sun. A few of these have already been named. How many more can you find to add to the list? Look in the *World Book Encyclopedia* under "Sun," or an online encyclopedia. Your school librarian will be able to help you.

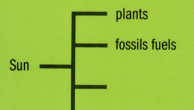

```
          ┌──── plants
          │
Sun ──────┼──── fossils fuels
          │
          └────
```

Fireball in the sky

You can see the Sun almost every day. But do you know how powerful it is? This massive, blazing body sends out an amazing and endless supply of energy in the form of warmth and light. The rays of the Sun transmit energy to plants and help them grow. We eat the plants and use the energy in them to operate our bodies. We burn plants to create heat.

In the same way, coal and oil contain the Sun's energy. Since they are **fossil fuels**, they are made of fossils that have been crushed and heated over millions of years. The Sun's heat also causes wind and rain and makes rivers flow. We can use the power from these forces for our own energy needs.

Coal, dug out from under the ground, is one of the most important fossil fuels.

Some sources of fuel have to be processed before they can be burned.
Equipment at this industrial complex extracts oil from oil sands.

Fossil or renewable?

As we have seen, fossil fuels like coal and oil formed long ago, deep inside Earth. Because they are so old, when we have used them up, there will not be any more of them. They are not **renewable**. We cannot make new supplies of coal or oil.

However, there are plenty of energy resources that will never run out. The Sun will shine for millions of years, winds will always blow, and rivers and seas will always move. We can continue **harnessing** (using) their power for as long as we want. We can also continue growing crops of new fuels to burn, such as wood and straw. These are all called renewable energies.

WORD BANK
harness   use the potential of something
renewable   fuel or material that can be grown and made again (such as plants from seeds)

A brief history of energy

Humans have used the world's energy for thousands of years. Until about 300 years ago, this meant renewable sources, such as firewood, wind, and water. Then came the **Industrial Revolution**, a period in history from the late 1700s through the 1800s, when factories, mills, and steam engines came into use in places like Great Britain and the United States. These new inventions needed much more power. Coal became the most important fuel, and huge quantities were dug up and burned.

The use of fossil fuels took another big leap about 150 years ago. People discovered how to turn **petroleum** (oil) into fuel. Soon gasoline and oil were being burned in cars, trains, and power stations. **Natural gas** was often found underground with oil, and this became another major energy source, used for purposes like home heating and cooking.

Carbon crisis

The world's production of coal has increased by 800 times since 1769, and it is still doubling every 20 years. Demand for coal, oil, and natural gas is going to continue growing in the immediate future.

But the amazing rise of fossil fuels has come at a huge cost. When they are burned, **carbon** is released into the **atmosphere**. The atmosphere is the layer of gases surrounding Earth that allows us to breathe. Most carbon forms the gas **carbon dioxide**. This gas is a major cause of **climate change**, the change of global and regional weather patterns.

The graph on page 13 shows how much carbon dioxide levels have increased.

During the Industrial Revolution, coal was burned to power steam trains and other machines.

Where are the main energy sources?

As we already seen, over 75 percent of all the world's energy is **generated** from fossil fuels. Demand is so high that coal, oil, and natural gas are worth a lot of money. But these things are only found in certain parts of the world. Some countries have grown very wealthy by selling their supplies.

Renewable energy is different. It is not in the ground waiting to be dug up. Generally speaking, water, wind, and solar energy can be found anywhere. But some regions have stronger sunlight, faster rivers, and more wind than others. They will obviously be able to produce the most renewable power. Can you find them on the map at the top of page 14?

Keep an energy diary

How many kinds of energy affect your daily life? How much energy does your household use? Why not start a daily log? You can use it to record what sorts of energy you use and how often you use them. You will be able to see what effect your own actions have.

You can decide on the layout of the log yourself, but you could divide the pages into columns— for electricity, gas, oil, gasoline, and so on. Then make a note every time you use one of these sources, and for how long.

At the end of each day, add up the total. Now record the reading on your gas or electricity meter. (Ask an adult to show you how to do this.) Compare the results with the day before, and over a week. Look for things that use lots of energy.

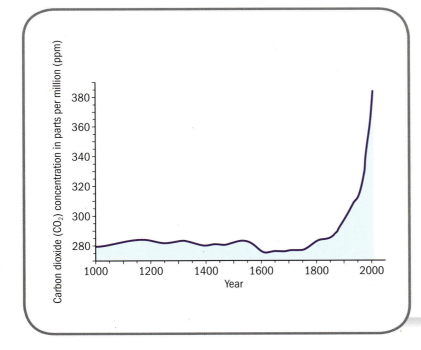

This graph shows the levels of carbon dioxide in Earth's atmosphere over the last 1,000 years.

WORD BANK

atmosphere	envelope of gases that surrounds Earth and allows us to breathe
carbon dioxide	colorless gas we breathe out, made of oxygen and carbon
climate change	change in the global and regional patterns of temperature, rainfall, or wind
Industrial Revolution	period in history from the late 1700s through the 1800s, when factories, mills, and steam engines came into use in places like Great Britain and the United States

Poorer **developing countries**, including many in Africa, South America, and Asia, have used very little energy. But now many of these **economies** are growing at great speed. Countries in these regions are building major areas with factories, power stations, and transportation systems, and they are also selling more cars and other goods. China, India, and Brazil are now among the leading users of energy in the world, much of it from fossil fuels.

Clean energy as a percentage of world energy use in 2006

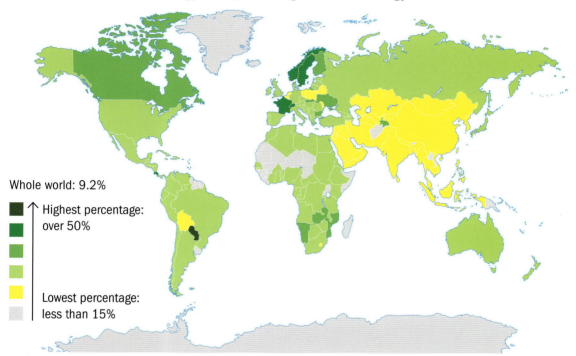

Whole world: 9.2%

↑ Highest percentage: over 50%

Lowest percentage: less than 15%

Fossil fuel use as a percentage of world energy use in 2006

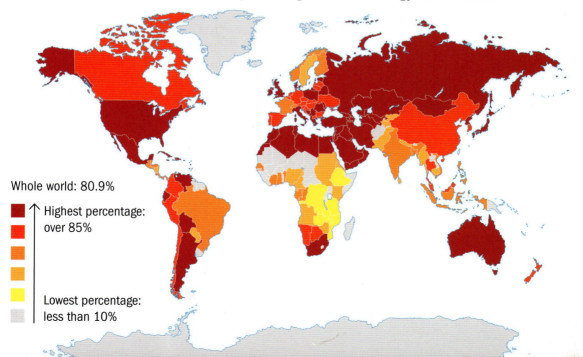

Whole world: 80.9%

↑ Highest percentage: over 85%

Lowest percentage: less than 10%

Pollution in China

Since the 1900s, by far the biggest users of energy have been **developed countries,** meaning wealthy countries such as the United States, Germany, Great Britain, and Japan. The United States, for example, contains only about 5 percent of the world's **population**. Yet it has used 26 percent of the world's energy.

China uses more coal than the United States and the European Union combined, completing a new coal power station every 10 days. It does so to keep up with the needs of its quickly expanding economy.

But the result of burning all this coal is **pollution** (poisonous or dangerous substances). These gases affect the health of people in China. They also affect people elsewhere, as clouds of pollution are spreading across the Pacific Ocean to the United States.

China is working to find ways to clean up its gas **emissions** (the exhaust given off). But the country must struggle to find a balance between the need to support its expanding economy and the need to keep the environment clean.

Coal burned in power stations produces gases that are dangerous to health.

WORD BANK

developing country	poor country where people do not have a high standard of living
economy	management of money and other resources of a country, community, or business
emission	giving off exhaust gases or other materials
pollution	harming the environment with poisonous or dangerous substances

Fossil Fuels

Coal, oil, and **natural gas** are an essential part of our lives. Just think of the things we probably would not have without them—cars, electricity, plastics, central heating, air travel, and more. But we know that burning these **fossil fuels** is endangering our lives by causing **global warming**. Is there any way to make them safer and longer-lasting?

King coal

The fossil fuel coal made the **Industrial Revolution** possible. Its **energy** gave us the power to use Earth's riches, and it brought wealth and plenty to many parts of the world. Even today, coal is one of the major energy sources, and coal production is set to increase in years to come.

There are two types of coal. The best-known type is hard coal, which is black and gives out a lot of energy when burned. The second type is brown coal, which is softer and contains less energy. Both have to be taken out of the ground, sometimes from very deep mines. Coal mining is a hard and dangerous job.

Can we make coal clean?

Coal is dirty stuff. When burned, it not only releases **carbon**, but also a substance called **sulfur** and other dangerous gases that similarly cause **pollution**. Can it be cleaned up? Scientists are developing a system called Carbon Capture and Storage (CCS). The **carbon dioxide** is taken out the waste gases from coal power stations. It is then pumped deep into the ground and stored under pressure. So far, no full-scale CCS system has been built.

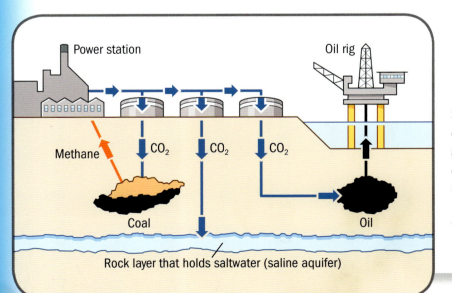

Power station   Oil rig

Methane CO_2 CO_2 CO_2

Coal   Oil

Rock layer that holds saltwater (saline aquifer)

Some people believe carbon gases from power stations can be stored underground. But is there room for it all?

Many environmentalists and scientists argue that the technology of CCS has not been proven to work, and we should not rely on it to solve long-term environmental or energy problems. Instead, people should try to change their lifestyles—for instance, by reducing their consumption of fossil fuels.

What would YOU do ?

Should countries pay for all the pollution that happens within their borders? Or should multinational companies that pollute the area pay for the cleanup? If so, how could you make sure this happens?

Cutting and moving coal out of a mine is a difficult and dangerous job.

CASE STUDY

The West Virginia mine disaster

On April 5, 2010, a huge explosion killed 29 miners at the Upper Big Branch coal mine in West Virginia. The explosion prompted many questions about mine safety. You can find out more about this story by going to http://www.cnn.com and searching for "West Virginia mining disaster."

Did you know that thousands of miners die every year around the world? See what you can find out about conditions in coal mines, and about the dangers miners face every day.

WORD BANK
sulfur   natural element that can pollute the environment if spread in large amounts (for example, from burning coal)

Oil from the rock

Another fossil fuel, oil, is the most important energy source in the world. Oil can be turned into many different forms—as fuel for vehicles and power stations, as the raw material for plastics, acids, and other chemicals, as a lubricant (grease) for machines, and as a surfacing for roads.

Oil's proper name is **petroleum**, which means "oil from the rock." It is found in rock or sand, often at depths of 3,000 meters (9,900 feet) or more. Many of these petroleum **deposits** (stores) are under the sea. Oil companies have to drill down into them from special floating platforms.

Black gold

The many uses of oil make it very valuable. It brings massive benefits and change to the **economies** of nations where it is found. This is why it is known as "black gold." During the last century, countries such as Saudi Arabia, Iran, and Venezuela became very wealthy thanks to their oil deposits. Today, oil discoveries are boosting other nations, including Nigeria, Libya, Indonesia, and Malaysia.

This is the city of Dubai. Many countries with oil deposits have become very wealthy.

Oil pollution

Scraping Bottom
By Robert Kunzig

Alberta, Canada— Once considered too expensive, as well as too damaging to the land, exploitation of Alberta's oil sands is now a gamble worth billions.

Nowhere on Earth is more earth being moved these days than in the Athabasca Valley. To **extract** (remove) each barrel of oil from a surface mine, the industry must first cut down the forest, then remove an average of two tons (1.8 tonnes) of peat and dirt that lie above the oil sands layer, then two tons of the sand itself.

The passage above is from a magazine article published in *National Geographic* in March 2009. The journalist was reporting about another way to get oil. Tar sands or oil sands are areas of sand soaked in oil. Extracting it is costly, messy, and does a lot of damage to forest areas. The environmental organization Greenpeace called it "the World's Dirtiest Oil." Do you think getting oil is worth the damage caused to the environment?

Can you find out about other places where oil extraction has damaged the environment? For example, you could look for information about oil spills, such as the *Exxon Valdez* or *Amoco Cadiz* disasters. Or there is the *Deepwater Horizon* explosion of April 2010, which brought catastrophe to the Gulf of Mexico.

It takes lots of water to get the oil from tar sand. Polluted water is then stored in special ponds.

WORD BANK

deposit	store or supply
extract	remove
petroleum	thick, flammable liquid (commonly known as just "oil") usually found beneath the surface of Earth

Natural gas

Natural gas is usually found wherever there are other fossil fuels. It is piped to the surface and cleaned of all impurities, such as sand and sulfur. Then it is piped to gas power stations and our homes for heating and cooking.

Natural gas should be one of the cleanest of the fossil fuels. This is because it releases much less carbon when it is burned. However, a lot of unburned gas gets accidentally leaked into the **atmosphere**, which can cause more damage than waste fumes.

"The world's annual production of carbon dioxide is 27,000 million tons (24,500 million tonnes). If this much were frozen into solid carbon dioxide it would make a mountain one mile (1.6 kilometers) high and twelve miles (19 kilometers) in circumference."

James Lovelock, environmental scientist, 2007

Energy into food

Natural gas is much more than just a fuel. Its energy can be converted into another important material: fertilizer. After treatment, the gas becomes a solid. It is sprinkled on agricultural land in the form of tiny white granules, or grains. These contain the gas nitrogen, which encourages plants to grow fast and strong.

The use of "nitrate" fertilizers like these has transformed farming throughout the world over the past 50 years. More food crops can be grown than before on the same area of land. In this way, fossil fuels are helping to feed the world better.

But there is a downside. The nitrates are being washed out of the soil by rain, and they are polluting rivers and ponds.

Some energy companies simply burn the gas they find with oil. This woman cooks food near the flames to protest against the waste.

If you were in charge of your country's energy, would you continue burning fossil fuels? After all, coal, oil, and natural gas are there to be used. Should we spend extra money to build new power stations that can "capture" the harmful carbon dioxide? Or should we stop using fossil fuels altogether? Is this a realistic possibility? If not, what should we do instead?

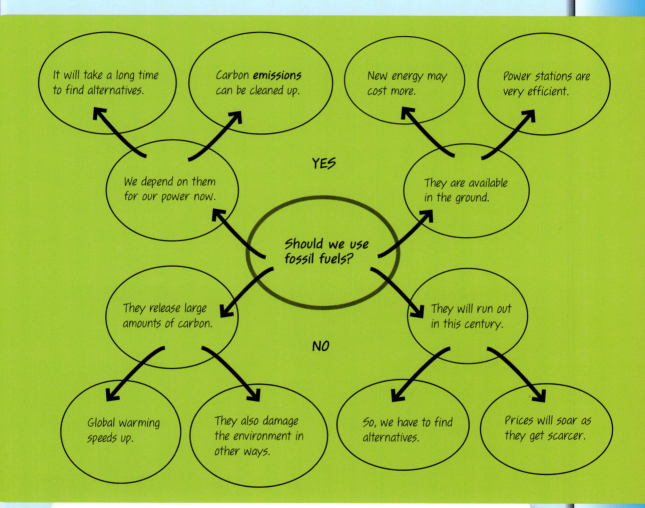

It will take a long time to find alternatives.

Carbon **emissions** can be cleaned up.

New energy may cost more.

Power stations are very efficient.

We depend on them for our power now.

They are available in the ground.

YES

Should we use fossil fuels?

They release large amounts of carbon.

They will run out in this century.

NO

Global warming speeds up.

They also damage the environment in other ways.

So, we have to find alternatives.

Prices will soar as they get scarcer.

A concept web helps you to arrange your evidence. At the center of the web (like a spider) is the main question. Arrows from this radiate outward, linking to boxes that contain possible answers. More lines branch from these, adding more details—or more questions.

Do your own research into fossil fuels. You will soon find lots of evidence. To help you make your decision, lay out your evidence using a concept web like the one above.

The Mighty Atom

Nuclear energy is the most powerful of all **energy** sources. It is created by the splitting of special **atoms**. (Atoms are the tiny units that make up **elements**, the substances that make up the universe.) This can create an enormous amount of energy.

Nuclear energy has been used to make the most terrible weapons in history—starting with the atomic bombs that destroyed Japanese cities in 1945, during World War II (1939–45). It can also be used to **generate** cheap and clean power. But how safe is it?

Splitting the atom

A nuclear power station uses the energy inside an element called **uranium**. The nucleus (core) of a uranium atom is split in two. This releases great heat, which is used to make steam. This, in turn, creates electricity.

A nuclear power station is very expensive to build, but cheap to run. It needs very little fuel. In a year, a nuclear power station uses only about 25 tonnes (28 tons) of uranium. By comparison, a coal-fired power station uses about 2.5 million tonnes (2.8 million tons). On top of this, nuclear power does not release any **carbon dioxide** or other waste fumes into the **atmosphere**.

Scientists check amounts of radioactivity in the air near nuclear power stations in case they reach harmful levels.

What are the dangers of nuclear power?

Yet nuclear energy poses big safety problems. Nuclear plants are dangerous places, because of the great heat and the poisonous materials involved. Mistakes can cause a major disaster. For example, at Chernobyl, Ukraine, in 1986, a nuclear station was destroyed in an accident. Deadly **radiation** (rays) leaked out into the atmosphere, causing sickness and even death in surrounding areas.

Nuclear power also produces dangerous waste material. No one has yet found a permanent way to dispose of this waste, so it is sealed in tanks and buried deep underground. But it will remain **radioactive** (meaning it gives off radiation) for thousands of years, and it could pose a threat to animals and plants. Everyone accepts that we need to find a better solution.

Many of the materials used to generate nuclear power become dangerously radioactive. They have to be handled and stored very carefully.

Where does uranium come from?

Uranium, like coal, has to be mined from under Earth's surface. Then it has to be crushed and cleaned, to get rid of all the unwanted material. These processes can cause great damage to the environment.

The biggest producers of uranium are Canada and Australia, which together provide nearly 50 percent of the world's supply. There are also large **deposits** in Kazakhstan, Russia, and Uzbekistan (in Central Asia) and Namibia and Nigeria (in Africa). As nuclear power becomes more important, many countries will want to make sure they have access to these areas.

Uranium mines like this one leave huge holes in the ground and cause damage to the surrounding ecosystems.

Nuclear power and France

In the 1990s, the government of France decided that nuclear energy would be its main source for electricity. It set out plans how it would research the secure disposal of nuclear waste, invest in advanced reactor development, and deal with possible fuel shortages.

Today, France's nuclear power stations provide about 80 percent of the country's electricity. That means France releases fewer harmful substances, like carbon dioxide, than many other **developed countries** and is less dependent on oil.

French scientists are now developing a new generation of advanced reactors, which can make their own nuclear fuel. They hope this means France's reactors should never run out of energy. However, France has still not solved the problems of what to do with nuclear waste.

Are the French right? What would you do if you lived in a country with few fuel resources? Would you risk building nuclear power stations?

Some countries, like France, are planning to build many new nuclear power stations.

Wind Power and Waterpower

Winds, rivers, seas, and waterfalls are a source of **energy** that will always be available. This is why they are called **renewable** resources.

Back to nature

For most of history, wind and water were often the best energy sources available. People made windmills and water mills to **harness** this power.

But, as we have seen, steam engines were invented during the **Industrial Revolution**. Along with coal and oil, steam engines could produce much more power, and produce it more reliably and quickly. As a result, windmills and water mills fell out of favor in wealthier parts of the world. But today, in part to save the environment, new kinds of windmills and water mills are being designed.

Many wind farms are built in the sea near the coast, where the wind speed stays fairly constant.

Blowing power

How do you turn wind into electricity? The first stage is to make the wind turn a giant fan called a wind **turbine**. Inside the turbine is a machine called a **generator**, which produces electricity. Wind turbines are tall, so that they can collect as much wind as possible. Some are as high as 90 meters (300 feet).

In wind farms, turbines are usually grouped together. The power they produce is fed into the main electricity grid (network). The biggest wind farms have more than 400 turbines and cover huge areas of land. Many are built offshore in the sea, where the wind speeds are stronger.

Is it worth it?

Some scientists believe wind turbines will never **generate** enough energy to replace traditional power stations. We also need other forms of renewable energy. Wind is free, but wind farms are expensive to build and maintain. Currently they provide only about 2 percent of the world's electricity. Many more wind farms have to be built to meet the growing demand.

Another big problem is that wind does not blow all the time or at the same speed. And some parts of the world get much less wind than others. Some people also think that wind farms are ugly and spoil the landscape.

What would YOU do ?

Imagine the government plans to build a big new wind farm near your home. It means that your region will no longer have to depend on electricity generated in a coal-fired power station. Is this a good thing?

Make a list of possible reasons for and against wind power. For example:

For	Against
It will make power cheaper.	Or will it make power more expensive?
It will not give off **carbon**.	The turbines will ruin your view.
Wind will not run out.	The turbines will make a lot of noise.

Use research to find more about this issue. Then make your own decision.

Waterpower obviously has a big future. But what is the best way of using it? Do some research to compare big hydroelectric projects like the Three Gorges Dam with much smaller, local projects. (Look on www.internationalrivers. org/node/356 or try finding a specific dam on Google Earth at: earth.google.com.) Which approach would you choose to provide a clean, safe, and efficient source of energy?

Falling water

The power of moving water can be used to turn a turbine and to generate electricity. This is called **hydroelectric energy**. It is now one of the most important renewable forms of energy throughout the world. Some countries, including Canada, Brazil, and Norway, produce nearly half of their electricity from waterpower.

Hydroelectric energy has many advantages. It does not create any air **pollution**. It is reliable, because water flows at a regular rate. The stations created to generate hydroelectric power usually last longer than other power stations. Best of all, waterpower can be used on both a big and a very small scale. Anyone near a river or even a stream can generate electricity.

However, generating hydroelectric power can also create problems. Damming rivers can destroy animals' natural habitats, and the reduced flow of water downstream can threaten fish and other water species.

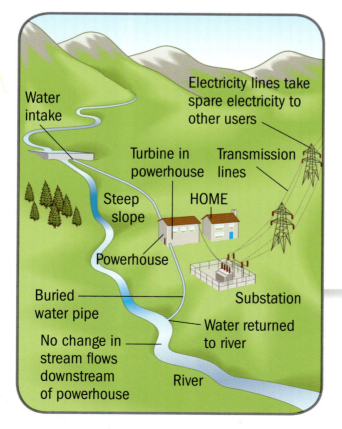

Water intake

Electricity lines take spare electricity to other users

Turbine in powerhouse

Transmission lines

HOME

Steep slope

Powerhouse

Buried water pipe

Substation

Water returned to river

No change in stream flows downstream of powerhouse

River

This diagram shows how the force of running water is diverted to the powerhouse where it spins the turbines that generate electricity.

The Three Gorges Dam

China desperately needs more electricity to help its towns and businesses grow. We have already seen how coal burning can cause major environmental problems (see page 15). So, the Chinese government is trying to find better ways to make power. One of them is the construction of the Three Gorges Dam.

Construction of the Three Gorges Dam started in 1992, forming a giant barrier across the Yangtze River. The dam provides hydroelectric energy and flood control on the river. However, the huge mass of water that formed behind the dam rises and falls. As a result, engineers have found that landslides and water pollution are more severe than they expected. The area near the dam is probably unsafe for people to live in.

In an article in the *Guardian* newspaper published on January 22, 2010, the journalist Jonathan Watts reported how 1.2 million people had already been forced to leave their homes, and how another 300,000 people must be moved. "We aim to decrease the human impact on the environment and restore the ecosystem," a Chinese official told the newspaper. "It will be hard because the plan will cost a great deal of money and involve finding new homes for many people." You can read the whole story at www.guardian.co.uk/environment/2010/jan/22/wave-tidal-hydropower-water.

What can be done about the pollution and the misery caused to so many people? How else could the Chinese have tackled their energy problem?

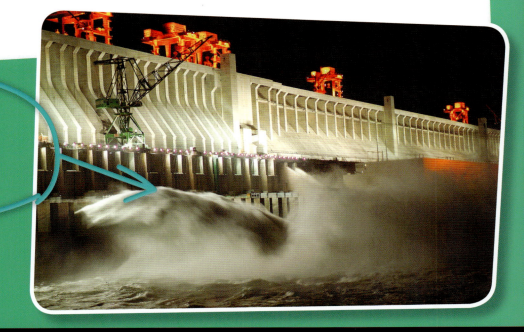

The gigantic Three Gorges Dam is nearly 1.5 miles (2.3 kilometers) long.

WORD BANK
hydroelectric energy   form of energy created when the power of moving water is harnessed to turn a turbine and generate electricity

Waves and tides

The sea is always moving. There are waves on the surface, caused by wind passing over the water. Scientists are working on ways to convert this up-and-down movement into energy we can use. Several systems have been tested on the coasts of Australia, the United Kingdom, Portugal, and other countries.

The sea is one of the most powerful natural forces in the world, but so far we have not found an efficient way of using its energy.

Most parts of the ocean have rising and falling motions called tides. The combined force of the Sun and the Moon cause the level of the sea to rise and fall. This movement can be used to generate energy. The natural flow of tides back and forth can be harnessed, so that it will turn turbines.

Developing renewables

At the moment, renewable sources provide only a tiny part of the world's energy. Why is this? For a start, **fossil fuels** are more convenient to use because the existing power system has been built up around them. Also, they produce a lot of power. So, energy companies have invested their money in mines, oil fields, and power stations. Very little has been spent on researching better ways of harnessing renewable sources.

This will have to change if we are going to bridge the coming **energy gap**. If we are going to use less coal, oil, and **natural gas**, renewable energies will have to fill the gap. Scientists will need to think of cheaper and more efficient methods of using wind and moving water to generate enough electricity for us all.

The new rise of British sea power

In 2008 a strange, 37-meter- (122-foot-) long device set off from a dock in Northern Ireland. The device, called SeaGen, was the first of its kind anywhere in the world. Looking like an upside-down windmill, it was designed to produce the first electricity ever brought ashore from British tides. Britain has the best tide and wave energy resources in the world. Official estimates suggest these sources could together provide one-fifth of the United Kingdom's electricity.

Can you find out more about SeaGen and other plans for using wave and tide power? See how successful they have been. Could these renewables really help bridge the energy gap?

This experimental machine uses the flow of the tides to generate electricity.

31

Sunlight

Without the Sun's **energy**, there would be no life on Earth. Happily, the Sun is only halfway through its life cycle and will probably last for another five billion years. So, it is certainly a **renewable** energy source.

Converting sunlight

There are several ways we can convert sunlight into useful energy. These include growing plants (see pages 36–37), heating water, and producing electricity from the Sun's rays.

Heating water

The simplest method of converting sunlight into useful energy is to place containers of water in strong sunshine. In some houses, a system of flat plates with water pipes running through them is used to **harness solar energy**. Water absorbs the Sun's heat and is pumped away and stored for future use. More cold water is then run into the pipes.

A much bigger heating system can also be built using this method. An arrangement of huge mirrors reflect the Sun's light to a single spot, creating enormous heat. This system is used to boil water and create steam, which turns a **turbine** to **generate** electricity.

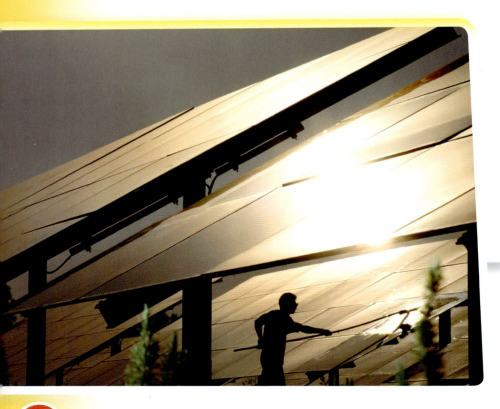

Solar panels with photovoltaic cells have to be kept very clean so they receive the full power of the Sun.

Turning light into power

Sunlight can also be turned directly into electricity, without using a **generator**. Special devices called **photovoltaic cells (PVCs)** convert the energy in the Sun's rays into a flow of electricity called a current. Sets of PVCs can be set up so that they automatically follow the movement of the Sun throughout the day.

Photovoltaic electricity is very useful in remote places where there is no normal energy source—for example, mountains, deserts, or out at sea. It also powers satellites orbiting (circling around) the Earth as well as other spacecraft.

Solar electric panels are fitted to the roofs of many new houses in sunny parts of the world.

What's the problem with solar energy?

The Sun's power is free, clean, and **carbon**-free. There is plenty of it, and it is unlikely to run out. It could solve many of our energy problems in the future, as scientists find new ways to harness it. Is there a downside? Think about these problems:

- There is no Sun at night. What happens in the dark?

- Some areas of the world (such as the equator) get plenty of sunshine throughout the year. But others (such as countries in the far north or south) get much less. Some get almost no Sun at all in winter.

- More satisfactory ways of storing solar energy efficiently need to be invented.

- PVCs are very expensive.

What would YOU do ?

How would you solve the problems posed by solar energy? Look on sites such as www.facts-about-solar-energy.com/facts-about-solar-energy.html for some ideas.

NK
aic cell (PVC)

Local power

One thing makes solar energy stand out from all the other sources. It is the fact that it is local. The Sun is on everybody's doorstep. Solar heating panels and PVCs make it possible for everybody to generate their own electricity at home, without complicated machinery or buildings.

Local energy can make a huge difference to our environment. Single households or small communities could make their own decisions about producing their own power locally. They would not need enormous power stations or networks of electrical towers and cables, and their electricity would be carbon-free.

Solar cities

Across the world, many cities have committed themselves to solar energy. They aim to increase their use of renewable electricity, though none will be fully Sun-powered for at least 10 years. These "solar cities" include Adelaide and Perth in Australia, Rizhao in China, and Seville in Spain. In 2009 India announced plans to increase use of solar energy in 60 cities.

What would YOU do?

Would you like your local city to become a solar city? Find out more about what this means. (Look on www.bettergeneration.com/solar-cities-around-the-world.html for ideas.) Write down your findings in two columns—"for" and "against." Then decide what you think should be done. Would solar power make your energy supply:

- cheaper?
- more reliable?
- more environmentally friendly?

People can generate solar power at home.

India's first solar city

The Indian city of Nagpur is being developed as that country's first solar city. Renewable energy sources will provide 10 percent of its energy, and there will be other measures to improve energy efficiency. Solar energy systems, including streetlights, garden lights, traffic lights, and solar water heaters, will be installed in the city. Energy-efficient "green buildings" will also be promoted. The central government will pay half of the estimated cost, with state or local governments providing the rest.

The Indian government plans to develop 60 such cities during a five-year plan, in order to meet the increasing demand for electricity in cities and to promote an increased use of renewable energy.

Several cities in Asia produce most of their electricity from renewable sources.

Fuels from plants

Plants need one thing above all—sunlight. Without it, they could not get enough energy to grow and produce flowers, fruits, and seeds for us to eat. But the stored energy of some plants can also be converted into a power source. We call these **biofuels**.

There are two ways of doing this. In the first method, fast-growing woody plants are grown, then ground into chips, and then burned in a power station to generate electricity. In the second method, the oils or sugars from plants such as sugar cane or maize are converted into a kind of fuel called **biodiesel**, which can be used to power vehicles.

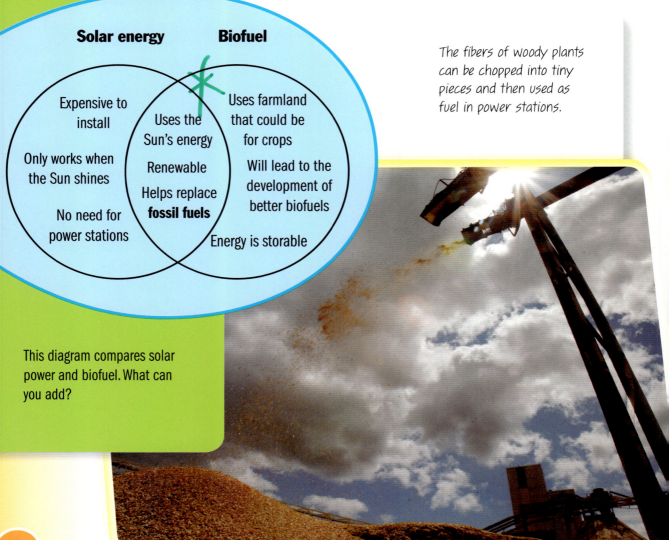

Solar energy   **Biofuel**

Expensive to install

Only works when the Sun shines

No need for power stations

Uses the Sun's energy

Renewable

Helps replace **fossil fuels**

Uses farmland that could be for crops

Will lead to the development of better biofuels

Energy is storable

The fibers of woody plants can be chopped into tiny pieces and then used as fuel in power stations.

This diagram compares solar power and biofuel. What can you add?

Miscanthus

A biofuel called miscanthus has recently received a lot of attention. This fast-growing plant is being grown in many countries as the raw material for a gasoline substitute or as a fuel for power stations. One hectare (2.5 acres) of miscanthus produces enough fuel to save up to 6.5 tonnes (7 tons) of **carbon dioxide** from being released into the **atmosphere** by burning coal.

Is it a good thing to use farmland for growing fuel crops? It means there will be less land for growing food. Surely we will need to grow much more food in the future, not less. What do you think? Do research on biofuels and find out:

- How much farmland is now being used to grow biofuels?
- How many people in the world face a food shortage?
- What are other ways to grow biofuels using the Sun's power?

Miscanthus (or "elephant grass") is a very fast-growing plant used for making biofuels.

WORD BANK
biodiesel   fuel made from natural oils that is similar to the diesel fuel used by vehicles like trucks

Energy-saving tips

We all need energy. So, we should all be responsible for how energy is used. We can do this right away, in our own homes. Here are a few simple tips for saving energy. Can you find more?

- "Standby" on appliances (such as the television) still uses power. Switch off the power switch and remove the plug from the outlet.

- Turn down your central heating by just one degree. You will save a lot in a year.

- Do not use a clothes dryer. Dry your clothes on a clothesline instead.

- Only leave your cell phone charging for a couple of hours. That is all it needs.

Less Waste, Less Energy

We have looked at the main types of **energy** we can use. But we cannot continue using them all. Some, like **fossil fuels**, are causing major damage to our environment. Others, like wind energy and **solar energy**, need to be developed much further before they can take over. Is there another way we can help to bridge the **energy gap**?

Saving energy

If you are short of energy, you have two solutions. First, you can get more energy from somewhere else. Or, second, you can burn less of the energy that you do have. That way, it will last longer and be less wasteful. There will also be less **pollution**.

To save energy, we do not just need fresh sources of power. Instead, we need to find more efficient ways of living. We have to make cars that use less fuel. Our buildings have to be **insulated** so that heat does not leak out. Lights and electronic equipment in factories, stores, and homes have to be used more sparingly. New materials and techniques have to be developed to make them more energy efficient.

This eco-house has a turf roof and is partly built underground to stop heat loss.

Inside an eco-house

An eco-house is a house designed to save energy. Everything about it is aimed to help preserve our environment. It is made from **renewable** materials that create no pollution. It uses water, electricity, and other resources as efficiently as possible.

Most of us, of course, live in ordinary homes. Many houses are old and were built before anyone worried about **climate change** or fuel efficiency. Yet even older houses can be made more environmentally friendly. For example, you can insulate roofs and walls to keep heat in. Or you can replace old light bulbs with new energy-saving ones.

Some modern homes are designed so that they do not produce any carbon emissions at all.

More ways to save energy

Here are some more energy-saving ideas:

- *Pavement power*
  The French city of Toulouse is planning to **generate** electricity using the tramping feet of pedestrians. People's feet will press down special pavement slabs, making enough energy to power the streetlights.

- *Cow manure*
  The United Kingdom's first power station powered solely by cow dung opened in 2002. It burns methane, the gas given off by the dung. The cows of 30 farms provide enough power to light 900 homes.

- *Giant kites*
  A U.S. company plans to build a huge kite, covering 1,200 square meters (13,000 square feet) and costing $2 million. This will fly above big cargo ships and help to haul them along. The company estimates this will save up to 20 percent of normal fuel usage.

The cargo ship MS Beluga Skysails was the first cargo ship to be partly powered by a kite.

Solutions big and small

On the opposite page, there are two case studies that show that saving energy can work. One is about a big, global company. The other is about a small, local one. Both have made big efforts to bridge the energy gap by using renewable resources and by cutting down on **carbon emissions**. Can you think of a company in your area that is doing the same?

Dell

In 2008 the computer company Dell met its much-publicized goal to be "carbon neutral." This goal can be measured by how much energy the company uses and where it comes from. The achievement was part of Dell's goal to be the "greenest technology company on the planet."

At the same time, Dell and a recycling company announced a new partnership to recycle any of the company's products (such as laptop computers) at Dell's 1,500 U.S. stores.

Many parts from old computers can be removed and used again in new products.

The Chipper

In 2009 a British company called First Bus began to use the Chipper. This is a bus that can run on 100 percent **biodiesel** fuel, which is made from waste cooking oil. This cuts down the amount of carbon emissions. In the first six months of operations, the bus cut the amount of carbon it released by 15,000 kilograms (33,000 pounds). That is the equivalent of taking 30 cars off the road for six months.

The company relies on donations of oil to keep the bus going. A number of businesses in the city have played their part and provided nearly 4,000 liters (1,000 gallons). Everyday people also contribute their own used cooking oil.

Energy: The Final Verdict

It is time to decide. How will you bridge the **energy gap**? Which kinds of fuel will serve the world best in the coming century?

Take a look at the sample tables on these pages and then create your own. Give each type of **energy** a mark between 10 (the best) and 0 (the worst) in each category. How do they compare? Do you agree with the figures below? Do some research before you begin.

The Local Impact

Energy Source	Cost	Sustainability	Reliability	Safety	Other Impacts	Total
Fossil fuels	8	5	6	2	1	22
Coal	6	3	6	3	2	20
Oil						
Natural Gas						
Nuclear Energy						
Fusion						
Fission						
Renewables						
Wind Energy						
Hydroelectric energy						
Wave Energy						
Biofuel						
Solar						

The column headed "Other impacts" gives you the chance to think how your choice will affect society. For example, if we close coal mines, what happens to out-of-work miners? And what about **developing countries** that have rich supplies of coal?

Finally you can add up the scores and find the winners. The table on page 42 is about the local impact of your energy choices. How will they affect us as individuals—at home, at school, or in the streets? The table on this page is about the global view. How will your decision affect the world?

The Global Impact

Energy Source	Cost	Sustainability	Reliability	Safety	Other Impacts	Total
Fossil fuels	7	5	6	2	2	22
Coal	5	2	3	2	2	14
Oil						
Natural Gas						
Nuclear Energy						
Fusion						
Fission						
Renewables						
Wind Energy						
Hydroelectric energy						
Wave Energy						
Biofuel						
Solar						

Glossary

atmosphere envelope of gases that surrounds Earth and allows us to breathe

atom smallest unit in an element, made up of a nucleus surrounded by particles called electrons

biodiesel fuel made from natural oils that is similar to the diesel fuel used by vehicles like trucks

biofuel fuel made from the stored energy of some plants

carbon one of the most common elements, it occurs in many forms

carbon dioxide colorless gas we breathe out, made of oxygen and carbon

climate change change in the global and regional patterns of temperature, rainfall, or wind. This can be caused naturally, or by human actions.

deposit store or supply

developed country wealthy country where people have a high standard of living

developing country poor country where people do not have a high standard of living

economy management of money and other resources of country, community, or business

element one of the many different basic substances that make up the universe

emission giving off of exhaust gases or other materials

energy ability to do work

energy gap situation in which we cannot produce enough power for our needs

extract remove

fossil fuel fuel such as coal, oil, or gas formed from the remains of ancient plants and animals

generate create

generator machine that produces electricity

global warming rise in the temperature of the Earth's atmosphere

harness use the potential of something

hydroelectric energy form of energy created when the power of moving water is harnessed to turn a turbine and generate electricity

Industrial Revolution period in history from the late 1700s through the 1800s, when factories, mills, and steam engines came into use in places like Great Britain and the United States

insulate add layers to a house (or a person) to keep the inside at an even temperature

natural gas fuel gas found naturally in the ground

nuclear energy energy made by splitting the nucleus (central part) of a uranium atom

petroleum thick, flammable liquid (commonly known as just "oil") usually found beneath the surface of Earth

photovoltaic cell (PVC) special device that converts the energy in the Sun's rays into a flow of electricity called a current

pollution harming the environment with poisonous or dangerous substances

population number of people in an area

primary source first or original source of energy, such as the wind

radiation giving off rays (from the Sun or from a radioactive material)

radioactive giving off radiation in the form of harmful particles, from uranium and other unstable elements, or from a nuclear reaction

renewable fuel or material that can be grown or made again (such as plants from seeds)

secondary source source of power that can be used, such as electricity

solar energy energy from the Sun

sulfur natural element that can pollute the environment if spread in large amounts (for example, from burning coal)

turbine machine that is turned by flowing energy, such as water, and that converts this energy into electricity

uranium element that is used to create nuclear reactions

Find Out More

Books

Benduhn, Tea. *Solar Power (Energy for Today)*. Pleasantville, New York: Weekly Reader, 2009.

Fridell, Ron. *Earth-Friendly Energy (Saving Our Living Earth)*. Minneapolis: Lerner, 2009.

Green, Jen. *Why Should I Save Energy?(Why Should I?)*. New York: Barron's Educational Series, 2008.

Guillain, Charlotte. *Reusing and Recycling (Help the Environment)*. Chicago: Heinemann Library, 2008.

Leedy, Loreen. *The Shocking Truth About Energy*. New York: Holiday House, 2010.

Morris, Neil. *Saving Energy (Green Kids)*. Mankato, Minn: QED, 2009.

Peppas, Lynne. *Ocean, Tidal and Wave Energy: Power from the Sea (Energy Revolution)*. New York: Crabtree, 2009.

Walker, Niki. *Generating Wind Power (Energy Revolution)*. New York: Crabtree, 2007.

Woodford, Chris. *Energy (See for Yourself)*. New York: Dorling Kindersley, 2007.

Websites

www.eia.doe.gov/kids
This website for kids offers lots of information about different energy sources.

www.energysavers.gov
This website tells you how to save money while making your home more environmentally friendly.

www.ecokids.ca
This website offers games, stories, pictures, and facts about the environment.

www.iea.org
The website of the International Energy Agency is a good source for facts and figures.

www.neok12.com/Energy-Sources.htm
Videos, quizzes, lessons, and games about different energy sources.

tiki.oneworld.net/energy/energy.html
An energy guide for kids, with links to other energy sites.

Movies

The Eleventh Hour (2008).
This movie, starring Leonardo DiCaprio, documents the dangers facing many of the planet's life systems.

An Inconvenient Truth (2006).
This film was part of former U.S. Vice President Al Gore's campaign to publicize the dangers of global warming.

The Truth About Climate Change (2008).
The famous naturalist David Attenborough travels the world to find shocking evidence of climate change.

Index